Contents

Introduction

Foreword

This book has been created to help levy-paying organisations in England implement a successful apprenticeship scheme. Quite simply, if you don't use the levy, you lose it, and that's a lot of wasted money that could provide benefits to your organisation, individuals and England. For your organisation, apprenticeships can potentially help you:

- Reduce spending on your training and recruitment budgets.
- Retain talent and reduce attrition rates.
- Motivate employees and reduce absence.
- Provide access to training or compliment your existing programmes.
- Promote and improve equality and diversity within your organisation.
- Develop the skills required in your organisation for sustainability.

On an individual level it can change apprentices' lives. Free access to training can open up so many opportunities: training can unlock talent that you didn't know existed in your organisation, and apprenticeships enable individuals to build a long-lasting career and increase their earnings. When thinking about the personal impact on apprentices' lives (e.g. attitude, earnings, home and work life balance, etc.), the personal impact of enjoying a job role, building a career and learning and developing new skills, are unmeasurable.

As you read further into this book, you'll discover the possibilities of apprenticeships. They don't just provide benefits within the bubble of your organisation or for individuals, they can also provide benefits for England. Apprenticeships offer an alternative route to education and training compared to traditional pathways such as college or university. Provisions need to be made for individuals whose strengths lie in vocational qualifications and opportunities to learn that don't end in debt.

As technological innovation continues to change our working landscape, what happens to the older generation who may need to retrain and change careers in the future? You'll learn in this book that basic skill levels in

England are lower than our neighbours. Your organisation could have an impact on wider social and economic challenges, helping England raise its education levels and provide access to learning and career development.

The current apprenticeship scheme certainly isn't the only answer, nor is it a perfect well refined process. As you read the chapter "Getting to grips with the Levy", you'll see how complicated the rules can be. This book is a practical guide, breaking down each step of implementation into short chapters. It's suitable for business owners, CEO's, HR and learning and development professionals, and anyone working in the apprenticeship arena.

Glossary

Apprentice(s) – these can be new recruits to your organisation or your existing employees. Apprentices complete various assignments, exams, projects, and training to complete an apprenticeship. Apprentices must be over the age of 16; apprenticeships can start after the final Friday in June that the apprentice has their 16th Birthday. Think of apprenticeships as another term for learning, developing, qualifications and training.

Apprenticeship Levy – a levy is a tax, and these funds can only be spent on apprenticeship training. The levy doesn't cover the cost of salaries or benefits.

Apprenticeship Provider – an organisation that supplies the training for an apprenticeship standard. This could be a college, university, or training provider. A contract of service is agreed and signed. Throughout this book, apprenticeship providers will be referred to as providers.

Apprenticeship Standard – standards relate to the new apprenticeships that have been designed by employers and approved by the government. Frameworks, which you may have previously called NVQs, will be phased out by 2020 and replaced by standards. Each standard has a specific cost allocated to it, called the banding limit. Where providers need to offer more support (usually with master's degrees), they may charge extra beyond the standard bandings. Extra costs cannot be paid using the levy.

Apprenticeship Scheme – during this book the apprenticeship scheme refers to the apprenticeships you implement in your organisation. Within your organisation you can call it an apprenticeship scheme or apprenticeship programme, etc.

Apprenticeship Training Agency (ATA) – ATAs help recruit and supply apprentices to your organisation. They are responsible for paying the apprentice, using their levy and managing tax and National Insurance (NI)

> Do not need ATA as we pay into levy.

payments, etc. The contract of employment is held by the ATA; your organisation does not fund the apprenticeship training (you cannot use your levy funds to pay for the training).

Digital Apprenticeship Service (DAS) – this is the government system where you can view your levy payments and deductions. Payments are automatically taken once you commit to a provider and commence the apprenticeship.

End Point Assessment (EPA) – this is the final assessment that all apprentices must complete to achieve their apprenticeship. This assessment is unique to all standards and levels and is dependent on the third-party provider that you choose to use. An End Point Assessor reviews the learning and evidence that has been met by the apprentice, which may include any of the following: presentation, panel interview, exam, professional discussion, observation, and project work.

EPA Organisation – this is a company that organises the end point assessment for your apprentice. They're an unbiased third-party organisation that ensures the apprentice has met the learning criteria. They should have no part in the delivery of learning during the apprenticeship. If an EPA is integrated (this is where the provider organises the EPA on your behalf), the EPA must be completed by someone who has not been involved with the apprenticeship learning. Integrated EPAs are usually seen within degree apprenticeships. In this book, EPA organisations will be referred to as EPAs.

Gateway – this process is managed by the provider. This process takes place at the end of the apprenticeship to determine whether apprentices have completed the learning criteria before proceeding to their EPA.

Levy Cycle – this refers to the 24-month period where you receive levy payments to spend on apprenticeship training. After the first 24 months, you'll start to see your earliest unspent funds leaving your DAS.

Talent Coach – called something different with each provider. Talent Coaches can also be referred to as assessors, subject matter experts, talent development coaches or mentors. Their support is covered by the levy funds and they're responsible for guiding and supporting apprentices. They should have regular contact with apprentices and ensure the learning criteria has been met. Talent coaches help prepare apprentices for their EPA at the end of the apprenticeship period, prior to the gateway.

Apprenticeship Levy

As stated in the Department for Education and Skills Funding Agency (ESFA) Apprenticeship Employer Rules: "An apprenticeship is a job with training. Through their apprenticeship, apprentices will gain the technical knowledge, practical experience and wider skills and behaviours they need for their immediate job and future career. The apprentice gains this through formal off-the-job training and the opportunity to practise these new skills in a real work environment," (GOV.UK, 2019 p. 6).

The apprenticeship reformation was implemented in May 2017, encouraging employers to participate and fund apprenticeship training in England. If your organisation has an annual pay bill of over £3 million, you're a levy paying organisation and 0.5% of your annual pay bill is tucked away into your very own government bank account - the Digital Apprenticeship Service (DAS); in other words, the apprenticeship tax.

The DAS allows the government to deduct the costs of apprenticeship training directly from your levy once you create an agreement with a provider. For global organisations, the levy only applies to staff in England; funding is only available if staff spend 50% of their working time in England. With regards to payments, only 80% of the cost of apprenticeship training is deducted from the levy via the DAS over monthly instalments throughout the apprenticeship period; the final 20% is taken after the end point assessment. The government also contributes a 10% top up to your levy, which you'll be able to see on a monthly basis on your DAS.

If you succeed at spending all of your levy, the government will contribute 90% towards the cost of apprenticeship training, up to the banding limits for the apprenticeship standards. Further details about the funding rules can be located on GOV.UK.

For levy paying organisations, the pay bill refers to payments made to employees that are subject to class 1 secondary NI contributions, which includes wages, bonuses and commissions. If you pay out a company bonus, for example in April, you'll find your levy amount increases the following month (e.g. in May). Any funds you don't use will automatically leave your DAS 24 months later. As the oldest levy payments are deducted first, you will always have a levy amount available in your account to spend on apprenticeship training.

The levy in your DAS covers the cost of apprenticeship training. It doesn't cover the areas listed below:

- Salary
- Benefits
- Travel
- Food and accommodation (some providers may include this)
- Membership with awarding bodies
- Exams (dependent on the apprenticeship)
- Extra services, e.g. recruitment assistance (dependent on the provider)

The above costs may affect how you allocate your training and recruitment budget alongside your apprenticeship scheme. It's likely, at the very least, that you'll need to pay for travel at some point during your scheme.

There are various apprenticeship levels available across numerous careers; to name a few, apprenticeships are available in: Construction, Dental, Digital, Healthcare, HR, IT, Legal, Leisure, Marketing, and Sales.

The information below compares apprenticeship levels alongside traditional education levels:

Apprenticeship Levels	Traditional Education
Apprenticeship Level 2	5 x pass grades at GCSE level, (equivalent)
Apprenticeship Level 3	2 x pass grades at A-Level, (equivalent)
Apprenticeship Level 4	NVQ Level 4, Higher National Certificate, (equivalent)
Apprenticeship Level 5	Foundation degree, Higher National Diploma, (equivalent)
Apprenticeship Level 6	Degree level
Apprenticeship Level 7	Master's degree

Apprentices should complete an apprenticeship at a level higher than the qualifications they already hold, unless there is clear reasoning for studying a lower level. For example, an apprentice may hold a degree (level 6) in Business Management and then start a Software Tester Level 4 apprenticeship. This reduction in level is suitable because of the change in subject, skill and knowledge.

Apprenticeships can be used in three ways within your organisation:

- Recruit new talent into the organisation.
- Offer internal vacancies to existing staff.
- Offer apprenticeships to upskill existing staff.

All apprenticeships last a minimum of 12 months and are supported by a provider. Apprentices are required to work a minimum of 30 hours per week, with 50% of their working time in England. Apprenticeships are available to workers who are either part-time or on zero-hour contracts, providing the funding rules are adhered to. For apprentices working below 30 hours per week, the apprenticeship period should be extended and providers can assist you in these situations.

A provider can be a college, university, ATA or training provider, and there's nothing stopping you using all four to meet your needs. Providers will allocate a talent coach to each apprentice; between yourself, the talent coach, and manager, the apprentice should have the right support and guidance to achieve their certificate and development goals.

All apprenticeships require 20% off-the-job training per week, but this time can be accrued throughout the apprenticeship period, providing better flexibility for your teams and diaries, e.g. a five-day training course equates to five weeks' worth of the 20% training criteria. The 20% can develop knowledge, skills and behaviours; therefore, areas such as presenting for the first time or displaying leadership skills can contribute towards the criteria.

The 20% learning plan should be clearly documented in a commitment statement issued by the provider and requires support from the talent coach and manager/team mentor. For existing members of staff upskilling through an apprenticeship, 20% off-the-job training can include anything that isn't part of their usual job, such as: listening to podcasts, attending workshops, completing e-learning, writing assignments, revising for exams and completing new projects, etc.

If you have an existing customer advisor completing a customer service apprenticeship, you'll need to plan their learning separately to their day-to-day role – maybe they can spend some time on reception and learn the complaints procedure? You can link the 20% off-the-job training to personal development plans.

 If your apprentice is a new recruit, they'll meet the 20% criteria quickly because everything is new to them – you might find the 20% requirements are logged within the first few months of their employment. It's still important to plan their development throughout the apprenticeship period and ensure they have exposure to tasks relevant to their apprenticeship standard that develops their knowledge, skills and behaviour.

The 20% off-the-job training criteria is based on the apprentices working hours, minus the minimum 28 days holiday entitlement including bank holidays. The requirements are adjusted for part time staff/zero-hour contracts, the calculation of which is located in the employer rules.

All apprentices should keep a learning log to show their 20% off-the-job training; this is reviewed by the talent coach and EPA assessor. This log can be a simple Excel spreadsheet, although providers tend to supply their own template, which is accessed and stored online.

Key areas to record are:

- Date of learning
- Duration of learning
- Learning acquired (detail of the knowledge, skills and behaviours)

Apprentices completing level 3 or above are required to hold grade C (4/5 points) in English and Maths GCSE (or equivalent) and where this hasn't been achieved, apprentices will be required to complete Functional Skills English and Maths Level 2 alongside their apprenticeship standard. This learning is covered by the levy and will be supported by your chosen provider.

Apprentices completing level 2 or below will also be encouraged and supported to complete Level 2 Functional Skills (level 1 may be acceptable where there are learning difficulties such as Special Educational Needs).

Studying towards Functional Skills cannot contribute towards the 20% criteria. If there's a break in learning, the 20% pauses, and where an apprentice needs time off for medical reasons or extenuating circumstances, the apprenticeship period should be extended. Your provider can advise you appropriately during these situations.

At the end of the apprenticeship period, a meeting is arranged between the apprentice, talent coach and manager, to ensure the apprentice has met the criteria and the 20% off-the-job training. Once this has been confirmed, the apprentice is ready to complete their final assessment. This process is called the "Gateway". The final assessment is called the "End Point Assessment," (EPA), which is only organised once the gateway has been completed and the relevant paperwork has been sent from the talent coach to the EPA of your choice.

EPAs are completed by a third-party organisation (separate to your provider) and the funding is included within your levy and your agreement with your provider. This process ensures the assessment is unbiased and confirms apprentices have met all the criteria. Every EPA has a different method to assess apprentices and this is unique to all standards and levels. Once the EPA is complete, the apprentice will receive their apprenticeship certificate and the final 20% funding will be deducted from your DAS.

It's easy to feel overwhelmed at this stage because the levy is complicated, particularly if your organisation is new to apprenticeships. This book breaks down all the stages so that you understand how the levy works and how you can *actually* implement and utilise the levy.

Alongside this book and prior to implementing an apprenticeship scheme, read the apprenticeship employer rules to ensure you're comfortable with the levy and your organisation is compliant. Important rules are highlighted below:

- Apprentices must spend 50% of their working time in England.
- Funding is only available to those eligible to work in England.
- Apprentices must have a job role and clearly defined responsibilities. Ensure you have a job description and contract of employment for apprentices.
- Apprentices must be employed up to the end of their EPA (relevant for non-permanent staff or apprentices from an ATA).
- Apprenticeships must be completed during working hours.
- If you're using the levy to upskill your existing staff, ensure the apprenticeship is broadening their knowledge, skills and behaviours.
- Apprentices already receiving funding from the Department for Education (DfE), may not be eligible for an apprenticeship.
- Apprentices cannot fund any part of their apprenticeship, including exam fees and travel costs.
- Apprentices should complete an apprenticeship at a level higher than the qualifications they already hold, unless there is clear reasoning for studying a lower level.

Be sure to check the employer rules on an annual basis to review the up-to-date versions. For example, the government provided clarity surrounding the 20% off-the-job training in the 2018/2019 rules. It provided more detail about how the hours are calculated, deducting annual leave from the hours worked. The 2019/2020 rules also provided more detail about the Functional Skills English and Maths. You may also want to review the provider rules (aimed at training and education providers) to check the service you receive is compliant. Set annual reminders in your calendar so that you stay abreast of changes during your apprenticeship scheme.

Why the Levy?

If you don't use your levy, you lose it. This book will help you make the most of your levy and implement an apprenticeship scheme that will provide a positive impact for your organisation.

Since the levy was introduced in May 2017, it's been a slow burner in terms of the information and support available to employers; the standards available for generic office and sales based roles were limited, whilst colleges, universities and providers were still finding their feet with the new scheme. It's only recently that the government has started to build bridges between local authority, education, training providers and employers, to improve the success of the levy.

The government's original vision was to increase the number of apprentices to three million by 2020. Since the 2016/2017 academic year, there's been a reduction of apprenticeship starts by 119,100 in 2017/2018, to 375,800. Confusion surrounding the levy has reduced apprenticeship numbers from its height between 2010 and 2012, which saw on average 500,000 starts per year (House of Commons Briefing Paper, January 2019).

The levy was introduced in response to the Richard Review, (2012) and the OECD report "Building Skills for All: A Review of England," (2016).   The Richard Review highlighted the complexity of qualifications in the existing world of apprenticeships and vocational qualifications, recommending a framework to test job competency, linking learning to practical skills. The OECD report highlighted how England ranked low in basic skills against other OECD member countries. The authors Kuczera and Windisch stated: "There are an estimated 9 million working aged adults in England (more than a quarter of adults aged 16-65) with low literacy or numeracy skills or both" OECD, 2016 p. 22).

The report findings highlighted that university students and those completing vocational post-secondary qualifications had lower basic skills amongst OECD countries; numeracy and literacy skills were low for those aged 16-19. The OECD report not only provided reformation plans for schools and universities, it also recommended improving access to valuable and meaningful workplace learning, to improve skill levels and education in England. Findings from these reports have contributed towards changes that now require students to stay in education until the age of 18 and apprentices to achieve Functional Skills in English and Maths.

Using your levy to introduce apprenticeships can positively affect productivity, attrition, absence rates and motivation. It can also close the skills gap that will inevitably affect every organisation in our ageing population. On a very basic level, the levy can help you reduce spending on your training budget.

Apprenticeship Timeline

Apprenticeships date back to the 1500s in medieval England, when apprentices would live with their masters for seven years to learn a trade. The Statute of Artificers in 1563 outlined the first rules for apprenticeships, informing masters that they could only employ three apprentices at one time (Commons Library, 2019).

Below is a brief timeline to show significant changes and the progression of apprenticeships in England:

1900s – Apprenticeships spread to industries like engineering and shipbuilding and were unsurprisingly popular after the World Wars.

1994 – Modern Apprenticeships launched for 18-19 year olds.

2004 – Apprenticeships became available to anyone over the age of 25 and rebranded as Advanced Apprenticeships.

2007/2008 – Annual apprenticeship numbers rose above 200,000.

2009 – The National Apprenticeship Service launched in response to the 2006 Leitch Review.

2010 – The government funded apprenticeships and during the academic years of 2010 to 2012, averaged at 500,000 apprenticeship starts each year.

2012 – Grants were made available to small businesses supporting apprentices aged 18-24. The minimum apprenticeship period of 12 months was introduced alongside the minimum requirement of 30 working hours per week.

2013 - Learner loans were introduced and covered half the cost for those over the age of 24 (learner levels dropped due to less funding).

2015 - Degree Apprenticeships launched.

2016 – The Apprenticeship Institute launched, working closely with employers to trailblaze new apprenticeship standards.

2017 – The Apprenticeship Levy was introduced.

Laying the Foundations

Resource

Whether you're the owner of your business, CEO, MD, HR director, head of learning and development or a senior manager, you'll need to allocate resources to ensure your apprenticeship scheme is successful. This, in itself, can be a great opportunity to develop the role of an existing employee in your organisation and start an apprenticeship (potentially the Learner/Coach or Learning and Development apprenticeship) – win-win!

To successfully run an apprenticeship scheme, you'll need somebody who can manage the below responsibilities (to name a few):

- Manage supplier relationships and contracts;
- Implement and share your apprenticeship brand;
- Plan and share communications – internally and externally;
- Manage apprenticeship recruitment (if relevant);
- Manage relations and expectations between providers, apprentices and managers;
- Record and monitor data and return on investment (ROI);
- Manage the levy and DAS.

Return on Investment

ROI is normally considered at the end of training programmes, when organisations want to see quick results and justify resources and spending. To implement an apprenticeship scheme, it's useful to determine where you want to see results and link this to your overall strategy. For a few hints on which direction you should take, answer the following questions:

- Do you want to save money from your existing training budget?
- Are you looking to reduce recruitment costs?
- Where do you want to see a return on training implementation?
- Do you need to focus on specific areas for the future e.g. digital skills?
- Have you recently completed a learning needs analysis or skills matrix that highlighted gaps in knowledge, skills and behaviours?

Once you have your foundations, you can then build a picture of where you want to spend your levy and monitor progress, e.g. attrition rates. Are you struggling to recruit specific skills? Are your middle managers leaving because there's no progression or investment to reach the next level? To help answer these questions, gather feedback from your senior leaders alongside quantitative data, including attrition rates, absence rates, recruitment costs, training costs, employee satisfaction surveys, learning needs analysis, and skills matrices.

Longer term, you might want to implement a process that allows managers to rate apprenticeship performance so that you can report on the success of skill, knowledge and behaviour development, and potentially compare their progress to non-apprentices.

Managers can use online questionnaires or a rating form to score apprentices throughout their lifecycle, right from start-up through to completion, and even a few years into their career.

Strategy

Once you've addressed ROI and highlighted areas where the levy can make improvements, it's time to align your apprenticeship strategy with your company strategy. What's the plan for the next two years? Are you growing your technology and digital space? Is the focus on driving sales and increasing brand awareness? Are you acquiring other organisations? Are you going through organisational design? By the time you review your ROI and strategy, you'll have an idea of where apprenticeships can support your organisation and depending on the size of your levy, you'll need to prioritise areas and test them out.

To ensure your scheme is successful and supported, it's important to gain agreement from your senior leaders from the beginning. The message needs to filter down to your managers and then to all employee levels. This task will be on your "to do" list indefinitely. Run workshops with your senior leaders to explain how the levy works and share your levy figure and strategy – the levy amount might sway their decision to support the scheme. Gather agreement about trialling the levy; it's important to find out what does/doesn't work in your organisation so that you can review your apprenticeship strategy at a later date. Trial several apprenticeships first before deciding the best fit for your organisation.

Managers/Mentors

You can manage, administer and mentor your scheme, in the sense that you're a liaison officer between providers, apprentices and managers. It's impossible, however, to mentor every individual, especially as your scheme expands. You're not an expert in every job role and qualification, and you're not close enough to every individual's performance and day-to-day skills, knowledge, and behaviour. You need your managers to be mentors, or even better, a senior member of the team who wants to develop their coaching and management skills (another opportunity to implement an apprenticeship – maybe a mentor, team leading or management apprenticeship?)

Before trialling an apprenticeship, it's important that the support framework is available. Your senior managers might be able to steer you in the right direction in terms of appropriate managers and teams who can run the first trials. This part is easier if you're in a small organisation and you're close to your colleagues. Depending on your training suite and culture, you might need to consider future coaching and mentoring training, ensuring managers and senior members of the team are equipped to support apprentices.

To speed things up for your trial, locate managers who possess the capacity to support apprenticeships and include them in the apprenticeship start-up process. Training for the wider management group can come later once you have more data and case studies to share. At a later date, you'll have closer relationships with your providers who can help provide this service and communicate apprenticeships across your organisation. Even if you just focus on one or two apprenticeship standards for your trial, the experience will provide you with valuable information so that you understand how it works and what future support is required in your organisation.

Trial and Error

You might not get it right first time ...and that's okay. The levy scheme launched in May 2017, but that doesn't mean employers, providers or even the government knew how it really worked; it's taken time for standards to be approved that are applicable to all types of employers and industries. It's also taken time for providers and EPAs to implement their new internal systems and recruit talent coaches and assessors.

Like any new venture, it takes time to figure out how it works and learn from those mistakes. When you launch your apprenticeship scheme, there's no harm informing your organisation that your first "levy cycle" will be a trial. You then have 24 months to see how it works, adapt and then cement the right processes.

Research

Speak to experts who've been involved in both pre-levy and post-levy apprenticeships. Locate organisations similar to yours in terms of headcount and job roles to see how they're utilising the levy (naturally, you might want to avoid direct competitors).

Attend apprenticeship seminars that provide the opportunity for you to network with local professionals (this is also a great way to increase your connections on LinkedIn). Grab contact details and go and visit their organisations - see their apprenticeships in practice. Find out: how they communicated the scheme, the challenges they faced, standards they're supporting and ask if they can recommend tried and tested providers and EPAs.

You can sign up to the government email notifications via the DfE. This will keep you updated about the world of education, which is indivisible from apprenticeships, especially for early year careers. Small changes might affect your recruitment and selection processes, e.g. the change of GCSE grades to a points system. It's also important to regularly visit the ESFA website to stay informed about apprenticeship news and useful webinars.

You can also sign up to email notifications via GOV.UK for the Apprenticeship Institute (this website is explained later in this book). This is a key website that should definitely be a favourite on your tool bar. Implement best practice and set a monthly or quarterly reminder to review the standards on this site. As your scheme picks up pace, you'll need to expand your knowledge of the standards available.

Digital Apprenticeship Service (DAS)

To set up your DAS account, you'll need your PAYE scheme and Government Gateway login details. Obtain this information from your payroll team (if you don't have this information, you can register for online services with GOV.UK). On the DAS, you can add other administrators to manage the system. It's highly recommended you provide system access for your finance director, payroll team and/or someone from the HR and learning and development teams.

Take some time to navigate the system; you might find adjustments are made as time goes by. Although some user-friendly tweaks could be made, it's an easy system to use and clearly laid out. You can: add apprentices, view apprentices, view your total levy, view payments, and add cohorts (allowing providers to add your apprentices to the system). These areas will be explored further in this book in the "Getting Started" phase. As you add apprentices and start to use the system on a monthly basis, you'll quickly become familiar with it. Failing that, you can contact the National Apprenticeship Service helpline on 0800 015 0600.

Apprenticeship Institute

The Apprenticeship Institute website will be your partner during the span of your role and/or apprenticeship scheme. Spend some time familiarising yourself with this website before you go any further in this book. On the apprenticeship institute homepage, visit the "standards" section to search for apprenticeships. The system is a bit clunky as you need to know the exact name of the standard to search for it, so make sure you're specific; it's sometimes easier to apply the level filter. You can find a list of existing standards using the "A-Z of Apprenticeships," (GOV.UK), allowing you to locate the exact title of the apprenticeship standard.

The Apprenticeship Institute website will tell you if a standard is in the development/approval stages and provides the contact details of the employers involved in the trailblazer (useful if you want to contact them for more information, e.g. release dates).

Once you've found a standard relevant to your organisation, e.g. software developer, you can click into the standard to view further information. You can find the cost of the apprenticeship, duration, the knowledge, skills and behaviour criteria, and any qualifications attached to the standard. Bear in mind that the duration of the apprenticeship is only the recommended amount and providers can sometimes deliver the apprenticeship in a shorter time frame.

When you're viewing a standard, you can also click through to see the details of the EPA and search for local providers in your area (via your postcode). This is a good time to start building your company apprenticeship prospectus. You might want to use a simple Word document until you know more about your scheme.

If you have access to digital programmes to build a prospectus, then you might as well start the draft at this point. A prospectus isn't just used to advertise apprenticeships in your organisation, it's a catalogue that you can use when you have conversations with managers and potential apprentices. It's helpful to have the information in once place, such as a list of standards available in IT, management, marketing, HR and accountancy, etc.

To kick-start your prospectus and make it easy for you to quickly find information, log the following information:

- Apprenticeship name, level, cost and duration;
- Website links to the main standards page and the EPA page on the Apprenticeship Institute website;
- Qualifications attached to the apprenticeship;
- Providers that support the apprenticeship – you can contact them at this stage to find out how the standards are delivered e.g. weekly day release or onsite learning.

Job Grade and Salaries

If you're trialling apprenticeships by upskilling existing staff, this section can always come later when you look at recruiting new talent; however, it's still important to consider career paths for all apprentices. You may need to liaise with your senior managers, reward and recruitment teams to agree the grade and salaries for your apprentices and their future development.

You might introduce a separate grading system and salary ranges for your apprentices. If you recruit three software developers on the same level in various teams in your organisation, you'll want to keep it simple, fair and consistent. You'll need to agree what happens to apprentices once they've completed their qualification and start to develop their skills to an advanced level. You can implement incremental grade and salary increases. Whatever you choose, it's important to provide clear development pathways to help your apprentices understand the investment you've committed to and most importantly – retain them!

When recruiting internally, grades and salaries can be trickier, especially if you're supporting long-serving employees. To help develop internal talent and improve retention, it's advised you advertise apprenticeships as qualifications, benchmarking grades and salaries with existing team members and within the industry. For instance, an employee with over five years' experience in marketing is unlikely to accept a role as a project associate if you're offering minimum apprenticeship wage. Speak to your managers, recruitment and HR teams to agree a plan and research what other employers are paying in your local area to ensure you're competitive.

Getting Started

First Apprentice(s)

The following steps can be completed in any order and you're likely to be spinning these plates in the air all at one time. To trial your scheme and in true apprenticeship spirit, simply "have a go". Depending on your organisation and the size of your budgets, some of these steps might not be relevant; you might outsource, but that can be timely and costly. Your scheme will evolve over time; therefore, it's recommended you don't make any permanent decisions (like embedding a shiny new HR/learning system) until you've explored all areas. Remember, trial and error, then cement your scheme.

From completing your "Strategy" and "Managers/Mentors" steps, you've hopefully identified managers who are keen to support apprenticeships in their teams. Research standards that might be suitable and then ask the managers to have conversations with their team (you can also identify potential learners through your performance review process). It's important that your first apprentice commits to the training, achieving their goals and providing you with your first success story.

You might want to trial an internal application form and interview process at this stage, it really depends on how well you know your managers and their teams, the interest you receive and how much time you have for this trial. It's worth considering this step now so that your future process for allocating levy funding is fair across the organisation and to all employees. You might find at this stage, prior to communicating the scheme, that you only have a couple of volunteers. As apprenticeships become popular, that's when you'll need a process for applications, sifting, and decision making. Some ideas to consider are below:

- Allow employees to apply for apprenticeships in your organisation, similar to job opportunities.
- Allow senior managers and your HR leadership team to approve requests (it really depends on where your levy sits – is it one

budget across your organisation managed centrally, or do you split the levy across your business units?)
- Set specific criteria for apprenticeship applications, e.g. performance ratings.
- Agree a policy and process for when you have numerous requests in the same team.

The detail for this can be agreed once you've had more experience signing up apprentices. Areas to consider when selecting apprentices include:

- Learning style – is an apprenticeship the right route for them?
- Timing – are there changes in their work or personal life that might affect their commitment?
- Previous education – depending on the level of the apprenticeship, do they have experience writing essays, completing exams and completing projects?
- Is the level correct – the apprenticeship needs to be challenging and achievable?

Like any vacancy, you can interview effectively and select the perfect candidate, but work and life changes inevitably occur. Apprentices might leave the organisation or find the level too difficult. Don't panic, you're going to come across these challenges along the way. The key recommendation is to ensure apprentices make the right decision for them. As much as you want to sign up apprentices, ask yourself if it's right for their individual circumstances? Your aim is to limit the number of learning breaks and withdrawals; the support outlined in this book will help you achieve this.

Sourcing a Provider

Once you've identified an apprentice and a subject, you need to source a provider. You can do this via the Apprenticeship Institute website and search your local area. You're not restricted to local providers because they can accommodate onsite training and/or offer blocked training at various locations. This is why it helps if you've agreed a training budget to cover travel and accommodation costs (when supporting 16 – 19 year olds, consider whether travel is suitable).

Speak to your colleagues because a lot of the apprenticeship providers were/are training providers and your colleagues may have previously experienced their commercial training. It's also wise to check Ofsted reports and follow your procurement process, checking service levels and their financial stability. The last thing you need is to go through this sourcing process again because a provider has dissolved two months into your agreement. Depending on the size of your organisation, you can request providers to apply through your procurement process each year or levy cycle. This can be a quicker and more detailed way of finding the right provider that matches your organisation – it's not just about finding flexibility for learning that suits your teams, but finding the right culture for your organisation.

When you've completed your checks and decided upon a provider, it's time to sort the contract. If you have a procurement and legal team in place, this stage can be fairly straight forward. You can draw up your own contract or review and sign the contracts given by the providers.

Below is a list of key areas to consider before signing a provider contract:

- Expiry date – when does the training relationship expire and do you need to diarise contract renewals?
- Is a complaints procedure and termination process included?

- Ensure exclusivity agreements are removed. Even if you're supporting one standard e.g. Marketing Manager, you may wish to trial a few providers to find what works best for your organisation.
- Negotiate an EPA re-take into the contract, you don't want to be lumbered with additional costs at the end of the apprenticeship period.
- The most important part – service level agreements. The support you and your apprentice receive is crucial.

Keep your options open for trialling more than one provider, even it's for the same apprenticeship subject. You might trial two at the same time to see which one suits your organisation. The levy scheme is still new to everyone involved; be cautious not to overestimate the capacity of providers and their capabilities. If the service doesn't meet your expectations (the enrolment process is slow and you find yourself constantly chasing for actions), these are the signs to trial someone else. Patience will be required though, acknowledging that everyone has teething problems.

Create a questionnaire that you can send to providers to help you make comparisons and make the right choice.

You can essentially ask providers to complete an application form, confirming:

- How they support apprentices, e.g. materials, training and online systems;
- Progress reviews;
- Your provider review;
- How they support the 20% off-the-job training;
- What is/isn't included in the levy, e.g. exams, travel;
- Services offered for learning difficulties;
- Minimum/maximum cohort numbers;

- Cohort start dates (some providers have set start dates throughout the year);
- Study days (are they weekly or in blocks throughout the year?)

Some providers may use a sub-contractor; check the details, pricing and support within the contract. A training company, for example, might work with a university to offer a degree apprenticeship. The main provider should deliver training at some point during the apprenticeship period.

If apprentices have relevant training/prior qualifications, the apprenticeship learning plan and cost from your levy can be adjusted. With accountancy apprenticeships, if an apprentice has a relevant degree, they could be applicable for exemptions in the Accountancy level 4 and level 7 apprenticeships. Check prior learning with apprentices when sourcing a provider and certainly ask the question because it could save you money from your levy and you don't want apprentices repeating their learning.

When prospecting for providers, it's worth considering the recruitment service they provide. Some providers can advertise your apprenticeship vacancies and assist with interviews, whereas others only support the learning. Depending on your trials and what support you have in your organisation, this might be a deciding factor. For more information, read the 'Recruitment and Onboarding" chapter.

You can now start to build your electronic filing system by storing your provider information and contracts in a specific folder. It's recommended you also create a spreadsheet (or use a system if you have one) to log your provider details. You can be very detailed, listing the specifics of each contract, expiry dates, contact information as well as feedback; this is the start of your preferred supplier list.

Within the cohort section of the DAS, you're able to give permission to your providers to add apprentices on your behalf (in the apprentice section). You'll need the providers UKPRN number, which they can provide. If you have a preferred supplier and plenty of apprentices signing up, this is a great time saver. Once you've given permission, your provider can add all apprentices to the DAS and you'll receive notifications to simply approve them – just bear in mind it can take weeks before the apprentice funding shows on your DAS and monthly deductions commence.

Sign-Up

At this stage, you've identified your manager, apprentice and the relevant standard. You've sourced your provider and you're happy with the contract/procurement process (in reality, the contract might be sorted behind the scenes, whilst you continue the sign-up process). It can take a few weeks to register an apprentice with a provider; this is why you're likely to be spinning all of these plates at once.

Arrange a meeting between yourself, the manager, apprentice and the provider, to confirm that everybody's clear about how the apprenticeship works, agree the learning plan and seek agreement that everyone is happy to proceed. During this meeting/webinar/phone call, you'll want to check the following areas:

- Dates of training;
- Talent coach support provided to the apprentice and you;
- Start date and the first progress reviews;
- Dates for your provider reviews;
- The onboarding process e.g. webinar or classroom session;
- The process for managers to review progress e.g. system access;
- System training for apprentices and managers/mentors.

Once the above is completed, you can start the paperwork with the provider. Apprentices must complete an Apprenticeship Agreement Form; you can use the template provided by GOV.UK. This should be completed once you have an official start date and store in your filing system. Create a folder for each apprentice or "learner" and ensure you save all relevant forms for audit purposes whilst complying with your organisation's General Data Protection Regulations (GDPR). You might want your HR team to manage paperwork relating to employees and apprenticeship new starters.

The provider should manage the registration paperwork directly with the apprentice and manager; it's up to you if you want to be copied in on this communication. This is recommended if they're a new provider, and you should keep talking to your apprentice to ensure they're receiving the right support and guidance during the registration phase.

All providers will ask apprentices to complete a commitment statement. For most providers, they do this via their online system. However it's done, ensure you have a copy and save this in your learner folder. This form outlines how the learning will be delivered and how the 20% off-the-job training will be met. These forms are important requirements as set out in the employer rules and they should be updated as and when the learning plan changes e.g. if an apprenticeship is extended or the learning is adjusted.

During the onboarding stage, you'll need to provide extensive support to your manager and apprentice, ensuring they have the right information, forms are completed, and the onboarding process runs smoothly (this stage requires a lot of chasing). This is your chance to note down feedback for the provider if you come across any stumbling blocks. It's also worth considering what support the apprentice and manager need at this stage. If travel or hotel stays are required as part of the training, who arranges this? If you're recruiting school and college leavers, they might need more assistance when completing these tasks for the first time.

Digital Resources

It's useful to have resources available for your managers and apprentices when they're going through the sign-up process, or even when you first start to have discussions about apprenticeships. It's a complicated scheme; therefore, it's useful to follow up conversations with further reading. Create a guide for managers and apprentices and be cautious not to overload them with too much information. Recommendations for content are below:

- Brief explanation of the levy (potentially a video of you explaining this).
- Brief overview of how apprenticeships work e.g. minimum 12 months, EPAs, etc.
- Outline the levels against traditional education they will recognise (e.g. Level 6 equates to a degree).
- Explain functional skills (relevant if apprentices haven't achieved the right qualifications).
- Checklist for managers – is the apprenticeship route the right development method for the employee? Can the apprenticeship be supported in the team?
- Checklist for employees – are they willing to complete assignments and potentially exams? Do they have the time and motivation to commit?
- Details about the 20% off-the-job training and examples of how this can be met.
- Expectations of the manager – support, mentoring, meeting the talent coach, etc.
- Expectations of the apprentice – recording their 20% training log, managing their diary and talent coach meetings, etc.
- Details about the EPA and examples of what this might include.

If you have the budget and resources, you can use e-learning or online tools to create these guides, or utilise your own marketing and studio teams to create branded electronic documents (this method is environmentally friendly and they're easier to distribute across your organisation).

In time, as you experience the whole levy lifecycle and have case studies, you can build more resources/e-learning, including: 20% training guides, mentoring apprentices, EPA guides and case study videos.

Brand

Brand is important to help you communicate apprenticeships internally and externally. You might want to use a different term for your internal brand because people still associate the word "apprenticeships," with teenagers on day release from college. You can call it what you like – qualifications, learning hub or training campus, etc.

You'll need to use your brand on your external careers site, intranet page and promotional material for events such as career fairs. As long as you're supporting apprenticeships, you can use the government apprenticeship logo. Visit GOV.UK for details on logo usage.

If you have a studio or marketing team on hand, they can help you put some materials together, e.g. colour pallet, PowerPoint slide deck, hashtag, leaflets, and stock images. If you want to personalise your brand, you can implement this stage at a later date once you have photographs and video case studies of your apprentices. Use this as an opportunity to link your apprenticeship brand to your employer value proposition, (EVP), promoting your benefits, culture, and working environment. As your scheme grows you can use various resources to share your achievements on social media.

Utilise your providers to share your great work and build your reputation, not only as an apprenticeship employer, but an employer who develops their staff. Some training companies have blogs and articles on their website, advertise the logos of their clients, and promote who they're supporting on social media. Liaise with your press team and find opportunities for increasing your external exposure.

Communication

As mentioned in the "Strategy" chapter, securing buy-in will remain on your to do list indefinitely and your communication strategy will grow and transform as your scheme expands. You might start out by meeting senior managers and implementing a few trials. Once you understand more about how apprenticeships work, you might then talk about apprenticeships in team meetings, talk to managers and organise events.

Agree a plan to communicate with your stakeholders. HR and Learning and Development Business Partners will need to be involved with apprenticeship conversations, not only to support the scheme, but manage challenges. What happens if a manager doesn't want to support an apprenticeship request? What happens if an apprentice isn't getting time during working hours to complete their learning? What happens if there are performance issues during an apprenticeship? Stakeholders around you are also likely to want updates about your progress. Can you attend leadership meetings or send a quarterly report/email?

Rely on the relationships you start to build; you don't need to be an expert in everything. Ask your providers, trial apprentices and managers to speak to other teams. You can even run Q&A sessions (a useful event to run during National Apprenticeship Week).

First things first, build a communication plan and align this with your trial apprentices. You can review this every six months or as and when your scheme changes and grows. At the start of your scheme, you might promote how the levy works. This might then transition to live case studies and then hopefully, success stories. You can look at blogs and videos from both the apprentice and manager/mentor perspective.

When you sign up your apprentices, ask if they're happy to be part of a case study, either internally, externally, or ideally both. If you don't have a marketing or studio team, consider permission consent forms that you can keep on file. As your apprentices progress through their learning, you can film updates and write blogs about their experiences. You can cover onboarding, 20% off-the-job training, support from providers, how apprenticeships work, mentoring, EPAs, career development and achievements. There are plenty of ways to build communication across your organisation; the important factor is to follow the journey of your apprentices and keep the momentum going.

Data

Once the sign-up process is complete, create a spreadsheet (or use a system if you have it) to record your apprenticeships. This can start off as a simple Excel spreadsheet and move to a technical system, if required, and providing you have the budget. Log the following information:

- Apprentice's name
- Job role/department
- Job grade
- Date of birth and current age
- Gender
- Start date
- Length of service
- Apprenticeship subject and level
- Apprenticeship sponsor, e.g. manager
- Mentor (this might be the manager)
- Apprenticeship start date
- Predicted apprenticeship end date
- Predicted Gateway date/EPA period
- Provider and contact details
- EPA provider and contact details
- Talent Coach and contact details
- Current status, for example, onboarding, on programme, EPA, withdrew, resigned, etc
- Result, e.g. pass or distinction
- Total levy cost
- Mentoring sessions – for both apprentice and manager
- Future career progression e.g. promotions and job changes

Some of the above information will come later, once you've organised the details, e.g. EPA provider. This log can help you create basic reports e.g. the age, gender and job level of your apprentices, whilst helping you set calendar reminders so that you're able to support the gateway process and EPAs. You can also monitor your scheme to check it aligns with your equality, diversity and inclusion policies. If you have a HR/learning and development system, you might be able to add this data to run reports and set alerts.

Although the DAS provides financial information, there isn't a page that gives you an overall picture; you need to click into each agreement to view deductions and then click into the deductions to view the apprentice they relate to. It's advised you manage your own system or spreadsheet to keep a log of the following:

- Monthly levy payment
- Monthly levy deductions
- Annual and 24-month total levy payments
- Annual and 24-month total deductions
- Monthly deductions for each apprentice
- Financial schedule for each apprentice, including final EPA fee

The DAS provides a forecasting area so that you can view clawbacks if you haven't spent your levy. You can also view your average levy amount for 24 months. It doesn't provide details; therefore, by logging the information above, it's all in one place to help you with reporting, planning, and conversations with senior leaders.

Mentoring

There are two types of mentoring for apprenticeships: the first is between the apprentice and their manager (or team mentor), ensuring apprentices have exposure to new tasks and time is provided to achieve the 20% off-the-job training; the second is your scheme mentoring, to check apprentices and managers have a positive journey.

At the start of each sign-up, add apprentices to your data log as discussed previously and arrange mentor meetings for the first quarter. Mentor sessions should be organised with apprentices and managers; the first meeting may be held together, but after that it's important to have individual sessions to effectively discuss performance and/or challenges.

It's advised you meet your apprentices and managers every month until you're confident they're happy, understand the process and the provider are performing effectively. You might then adjust your mentor sessions to every quarter. These can easily be completed via telephone/Skype if your apprentices and managers are offsite, although face-to-face sessions should occur where possible.

It's important to remind you that team mentoring sessions are crucial either with the manager or a senior member of the team. The mentor should meet apprentices regularly, linking their learning to day-to-day experiences, embedding performance and career conversations in regular updates. Your mentoring sessions are more like a temperature check for the scheme — remember, you're the liaison officer between all parties.

Create a review form so that you can keep a record of your conversations and actions, which is particularly useful when the number of apprentices increases. This is a key requirement of the apprenticeship employer rules. Do your managers have an update and review form to use? If you have a system that can log this information, even better.

These sessions are also a great way for you to learn more about each standard and level, building your knowledge as you progress through the scheme. The purposes of your mentoring sessions are to:

- Gather onboarding feedback;
- Confirm the apprentice has received contact from their talent coach;
- Confirm the apprentice has received their learning plan and everything is running smoothly;
- Conduct regular temperature checks to ensure apprentices: are booking their exams (if relevant), have regular contact with their talent coach, are logging their 20% off-the-job training and have support to study during working hours.

Your apprenticeship scheme should be a constant flow of communication between yourself, apprentice, manager/mentor and provider. This helps to reduce situations where apprentices require a break in their learning or withdraw from their apprenticeship.

You might come across a time when apprentices need to pause their programme. This can happen for numerous reasons, whether personal circumstances or related to the role, e.g. structure changes. Breaks in learning do not include sickness absence that lasts four weeks or under. Make sure you inform the apprenticeship provider if a break in learning is required so that they can pause the programme and levy deductions. You'll need to update the DAS in the apprentice section (you can click on an individual and edit their record). This is where you can pause a learner and input the effective date. You can start the funding again, if required.

Whatever the reason, it's important to keep in contact with your apprentice to determine if they're likely to continue and succeed. An apprentice may struggle if they're new to learning, but hopefully these signs and challenges will be picked up in your mentoring sessions.

To withdraw an apprentice, similar to above, inform the provider and update the DAS. Update your log so that you have information for the future, including the total number of apprenticeship starts, achievers, breaks in learning, extensions, withdrawals and leavers. You can learn from these situations; find out why the apprentice paused/stopped, e.g. did they have enough information at the beginning? Did they have enough support to achieve the 20% training? Do you need to adjust your application process?

If you're dismissing an apprentice due to performance, conduct or redundancy, guidance suggests that you can follow your company policies and procedures. There's debate around what constitutes a traditional or modern apprenticeship; therefore, it's advised you seek legal guidance in these circumstances.

The employer rules provide information surrounding changes in circumstances, summarised below:

- If an apprentice changes the apprenticeship subject, a new commitment statement, funding and learning programme will be required. Funding will stop on the DAS and a new agreement must be arranged. This might happen if an apprentice changes role within your organisation, e.g. an employee may stop a Project Management Level 4 apprenticeship and start an Operations Manager Level 5 apprenticeship.
- If you simply change provider and the apprenticeship subject/level remain unchanged, there should be no disruption to the apprentice's learning, besides paperwork and the enrolment period. Check your provider contracts before doing anything and all final payments must be made to the previous provider.
- If an apprentice is made redundant, the government will fund up to 12 weeks of the training.
- During redundancy, employers must provide support to apprentices to find alternative employment and training.

Further details can be found in the Apprenticeship Technical Funding Guide (April 2019 – March 2020).

End Point Assessments (EPA)

Although the EPA is at the end of the apprenticeship period, it's wise to source an organisation during the sign-up process. Although the standards are the same, no matter what provider you use, the EPA can differ vastly. This is where your contacts come in handy. Ask for recommendations for proven EPAs (you can access a list of EPAs on GOV.UK).

When you sign up a trial apprentice, check whether the EPA is integrated (this is where an apprenticeship provider works in partnership with an EPA and the assessments are arranged on your behalf, e.g. accountancy EPA's are conducted by CIMA/ACCA). Degree apprenticeships are also integrated. It's always worth checking because it saves you time.

Similar to sourcing a provider, it's recommended you follow your procurement, legal and review processes prior to signing contracts (the contracts are usually much shorter and simpler than sourcing an apprenticeship provider). The key thing at this stage is to obtain the EPA toolkits and overview to determine what's included and what support is offered to the apprentice. For a customer service apprenticeship, one EPA might request a professional discussion and observation, whereas a different EPA might request an additional presentation or written report.

It's key to find out this information and decide on an EPA early on into the apprenticeship period to ensure apprentices are aware of expectations. Similar to apprenticeship providers, you might want to use a questionnaire to find out what's involved. Make sure the EPA process is as easy and as smooth as possible for your apprentices. EPAs should have resources available to help apprentices prepare for their final assessment (time is allocated for this after the Gateway process). Check that they have videos, workbooks, templates and mock tests (if applicable).

Complaints

If you come across poor service levels from your providers, you can raise a formal complaint. There should be a complaints procedure in your contract to follow first and if this is unresolved, you can then raise a complaint with the ESFA by calling 08000 150400 or emailing nationalhelpdesk@apprenticeships.gov.uk. The apprenticeship helpline should also be made available to all apprentices. You might want to include this in your apprentice guide and/or intranet page.

You'll have regular opportunities to provide feedback on your providers through the DAS. The government will email you links to rate your providers. You can't provide any comments, but you can provide ratings.

Systems and Processes

As you complete your trials, you'll need to start thinking about your systems and frameworks, automating as much as possible so that you can run the scheme with high apprenticeship numbers. You might be able to think of quick fixes in your existing system or start to think about what you need for the future. You don't need to spend thousands on a system, for example you can use Excel, but you might need extra resource as your scheme expands. This could be a great opportunity to recruit an apprentice, maybe a Data Analyst?

Whether additional areas on your HR/recruitment system, or tabs on a spreadsheet, you'll want to be able to report on the following:

- Number of apprentices
- Gender
- Age
- Apprenticeship standard and level
- Status (on programme, withdrawal, etc)
- Result on completion
- Achievers, completers and leavers, etc
- Apprenticeship start date and end dates
- Levy spending

You can use a system or calendar reminders to set up notifications, reminding you when it's time for the gateway process and when an EPA is due. You might also want to set reminders to prompt follow-up conversations with apprenticeship achievers and their managers for the "what happens next?" conversation.

Create draft processes as you start your trials and involve relevant stakeholders to make sure you don't miss important tasks. Liaise with your legal and HR teams to make sure the contract process is compliant. Can you automate an apprenticeship pack to go out with offer letters and contracts?

You might need to create checklists and process maps to make sure you follow the right procedures for all situations e.g. internal apprentices, external apprentices and employee's upskilling. How do you record qualifications on your HR system? What letter templates need to be designed? How are payroll informed (your organisation can save money on NI contributions for apprentices aged 18 – 25, under the higher tax rate). The following checklists are recommended:

- Sourcing a provider (including EPA)
- Vacancy checklist – internal and external
- New starter checklist
- Employee upskilling checklist
- Gateway and EPA checklist
- Completion checklist

Checklists and process maps can be updated and perfected once you've experienced the whole levy cycle. Keep regular contact with your stakeholders to ensure nothing gets missed. As previously mentioned, it's a complicated scheme with various parts to it, so these checklists can prove useful.

Recruitment and Onboarding

Recruitment and Selection

Whether this is relevant for your trials, or your future scheme, at some point you're likely to recruit internally/externally for apprentices. According to Adzuna, in July 2019, there were over 28,000 advertised apprenticeship vacancies in the UK. Everything covered in the "Getting Started" chapter still applies; you need managers/mentors who can support the apprentice, the right standard that matches the job role, and you need to source a provider. There are, however, a few extra areas that you need to consider before recruiting.

When recruiting for an internal role, you might want to advertise it as an opportunity to achieve a qualification, rather than calling it an apprenticeship. Review existing salaries in the team and conduct external salary reviews to ensure the salary is pitched at the right level. For all vacancies, check:

- Grade and salary - ensure consistency across your organisation;
- Contract and offer pack – do you need a revised version for external recruits and internal movers;
- Recruitment and selection process – you'll need to adjust your job descriptions, interview questions and tests, etc.

You'll need to adjust your job advertisements, job descriptions, and selection process because you're not expecting apprentices to have extensive experience. You're looking for drive, interest and an ability to learn. You might want to trial one external recruit before the levy is used more widely in your recruitment plan.

Check annually for the minimum wage requirements as this is likely to change during the annual budget. The current minimum wage is £3.90 per hour for those under the age of 19, or those aged 19 and in their first year of their apprenticeship. After this, the specific minimum rates for age apply.

Visit GOV.UK for more information. It's recommended you research apprenticeship roles in your area to check your salaries are competitive – if you want to recruit great apprentices and retain them, you need to pay above the minimum wage.

Job Descriptions

Create a template that you can use for future vacancies. Build the first one with the help of the manager and your recruitment team. Change the language so that rather than asking for experience, you're asking for an understanding or interest, e.g. for a software developer apprenticeship, you might ask that applicants have knowledge of various languages, but you're not necessarily expecting them to have used them.

Include requirements that are specific to the apprenticeship to provide full clarity on expectations. Insert information about the 20% training log, booking assessment meetings and completing assignments. Do you need to include travel? Will apprentices be offsite for their learning?

Advertising

Some providers can advertise your vacancy and manage the applications, from sifting CVs right through to interviewing on your behalf, or taking part in your interview panel. If you're using an education provider to deliver your apprenticeship e.g. a local college, you can only advertise your vacancy through them; you cannot advertise through other colleges or universities. If training providers support recruitment, they will advertise your vacancy on your behalf, including the GOV.UK website, and naturally, you can use your own careers site and social media alongside this service.

Not all providers offer a recruitment service. In this situation, you can advertise your vacancies on the GOV.UK website yourself via the DAS (this is free and non-mandatory). This process is fairly simple – when you log into the DAS, you'll see a "recruit" tab where you can start to post your vacancy. You'll be prompted to add the relevant information, e.g. standard, duration, salary and hours, etc.

When writing advertisements for your careers site and social media, refer to the apprenticeship employer rules. It's essential you include the standard name, working hours and apprenticeship length. You *can* be specific about the level or you can keep it generic because it depends on the calibre of applications you receive. You might advertise for a Customer Service Practitioner Level 2 apprentice, but find that a candidate is ready to complete the Customer Service Specialist Level 3. You might interview a candidate for a Software Developer Level 4 apprenticeship, but then find the level 3 is more suitable.

You can use recruitment agencies for apprenticeships; research agencies that have experience with apprentices and have good reviews. There might be specific apprenticeship services in your local area that target specific audiences such as college students and specialise in early careers.

If you have the budget, it might be worth trialling these as it can help you sift candidates and speed up your process, saving you some time to focus on other areas.

Eligibility

Your provider should offer an eligibility check as part of their service, whether they assist your recruitment or not. This should form part of your selection process. Once you have selected your candidate(s), your provider can run eligibility checks to make sure the standard and level are suitable; this can be a simple phone call. Inform your applicants at the start of the recruitment process that this stage will take place before an offer is made.

Interviewing

Unless your managers/mentors are apprenticeship experts, it's essential you play a part during the interviewing process to explain the learning to candidates; you can discuss the apprenticeship during telephone/Skype interviews, or you can meet candidates at the end of their interview if you can't be on the panel. In the future, as your managers become more experienced at supporting apprenticeships, you can relinquish this responsibility. Consider interview guides and apprenticeship recruitment workshops for managers.

If you want to test candidates, remember to adjust them to suit the experience level. You might want to test how they make decisions and communicate, rather than testing technical ability or knowledge. Assessment days can prove useful, not only to condense your interviewing time, but also facilitate fun team games to assess specific skills and behaviours, e.g. listening, communication and teamwork.

Ensure your job description, advertisement and interview process match in terms of what knowledge, skills and behaviours you're expecting the candidates to display. This will help you produce a scoring sheet. Utilise the apprenticeship standard and your job description to design interview questions.

Using tests/tasks and scoring sheets during your selection process will provide valuable data to help you make a decision and provide feedback to candidates. How do you explain why a candidate was unsuccessful when you're not expecting them to have experience? A clear recruitment process, interview questions and scoring process will help you make the right decision and provide valuable feedback to candidates.

Feedback

The apprentice's journey is an important one – you want unsuccessful candidates, like any standard vacancy, to walk away with a positive view of your organisation and apply for other roles in the future, or continue/become a customer. Your apprentices might be new to interviewing; therefore, it's even more important that they receive structured, honest and constructive feedback to set them up for success in the future. If they answered their phone during an assessment day: tell them. If they struggled to answer questions: tell them. If they made grammar mistakes on their application: tell them.

Onboarding

When you select the right apprentice, it's important to give them full support from the date you offer, right through to their induction and first few weeks in their role. If you're recruiting early careers, it's very important to keep in contact with your apprentices and provide information that will help them settle into their first working environment. Apprentices have a new role, team and culture to adjust to, as well as studying. Depending on the time between the offer and start date, you and the manager might want to phone apprentices to check they're happy before they start. Can they meet the team before they start, or do you have any social events coming up that they can attend?

You can create a welcome guide for your externally recruited apprentices and your internal apprentices who are upskilling. This sets out expectations from the start and welcomes them to your scheme. Areas you might want to consider are:

- Next steps – what happens when they start?
- Reminder or links to your guides about expectations, 20% off-the-job training and the EPA.
- Contact details in case they have any questions.
- In the future, you might want to add contact details of existing and past apprentices who may act as champions, mentors and ambassadors within your organisation.
- For external recruits, you may need to cover basics like office dress, parking, the first week, where to have lunch and so forth (if not already covered in your offer process).
- Is support available when they start, for example if they have concerns or have learning difficulties?

Apprentices should attend your regular induction. A separate apprenticeship induction/meet and greet can take place additionally during their first week. The apprenticeship induction only needs to be one or two hours long and should recap information you have already provided at interview and offer stages e.g. how the apprenticeship works and the training involved. This is also a great chance to get the apprentice and team mentor together and show that support is provided from the very beginning.

You can go one step further with your apprentices and provide a welcome bag once they've joined. This may include: a card that welcomes them to the organisation, a contact list including their mentor and talent coach, notebook, pen, book or kindle voucher and maybe some company branded items like headphones and a reusable coffee cup.

With reference to the "Getting Started" chapter, it can take time to complete the enrolment process and apprentices to receive their training dates and contact from their talent coach. It's essential that you continue contact and meetings after the induction until the apprenticeship is fully in motion to ensure it's a success and everyone experiences a positive journey.

Apprenticeship Completions

Gateway and EPA

The Gateway and EPA is different for every subject and level. Some apprentices might be working on their EPA prior to the gateway meeting, for example, creating presentations, writing reflective statements and/or revising for exams. Others involve project work after the gateway. Either way, expectations should have been explained at the start of the apprenticeship period when an EPA organisation was sourced.   At the end of the apprenticeship, the EPA will be involved with assessments and preparation because the talent coach must remain impartial to this process.

The gateway is effectively confirmation from the provider and talent coach that the relevant learning criteria has been met and the apprentice is ready to complete their EPA. The Gateway will usually involve a conversation between talent coaches and managers; managers will be required to sign forms and confirm that learning and the 20% off-the-job training has been completed. The forms will be sent to the EPA of your choice to start the process.

Similar to the enrolment process, you'll be chasing contact, actions, meetings and support from both the provider and EPA during this stage. This is why it's important to diarise the expected end date for apprentices, making sure your diary is clear to offer full support. Although the talent coach cannot provide assistance, you and managers/team mentors can. If the apprentice needs to design a presentation, can you be the practice audience? Apprentices are likely to be nervous at this stage; therefore, it's important to meet them regularly, review their EPA work and provide learning support - do you have workbooks, videos, guides and/or e-learning available? Hopefully your EPA can offer these resources as part of their service.

You'll need to make sure the EPA is booked in the team's diary because it may involve a job role observation. The EPA professional discussions can also last up to ninety minutes. Check the EPA is booked around holidays/absences and full attention can be given to apprentices during this time.

Sharing Results

Once the EPA has been completed, it can take a few weeks to receive the results; the certificate will then follow. Where exams are involved, the results can take longer and there may be separate certificates for qualifications. Either way, make a fuss of your achievers. Shout about your successful apprentices internally, on social media and start filming those case studies! In the future, you might even consider apprenticeship ceremonies and "apprentice of the year awards," (you can also enter external awards). Whatever your process, make sure all your stakeholders are involved and update your data for reporting purposes.

Meet with apprentices and managers at the end of the apprenticeship to review the programme and obtain feedback (you can use an online system to send questionnaires). A final review is important so that you can consider the areas listed below:

- Salary increase
- Career progression
- Is further learning required?
- Is a higher-level apprenticeship suitable?
- Obtain feedback on the programme
- If relevant, does the apprentice want to join the Young Apprenticeship Ambassador Network (YAAN?)
- Can they get involved with events, for example National Apprenticeship Week?
- Can they act as a mentor?
- Are they happy to share their story internally/externally?

Building an Apprenticeship Culture

Support

Depending on the resources you have available, you can build your internal support for apprentices and their 20% off-the-job training. There's no reason why the support you build for apprentices can't be used universally within your organisation. You can build short courses that focus on soft skills and behaviours, e.g. confidence building, presenting, leadership and influencing skills. You can also add specific items to help those returning to study e.g. exam advice and report writing. If you have a learning management system, you can design/add a section specifically for apprentices.

Whether you recruit apprentices or upskill existing employees, it can be difficult returning to study. Creating a "back to study" programme can help support apprentices from the very beginning and contribute to your scheme's achievement success and distinction awards. A "back to study" programme can involve a blended approach, with online and face to face learning. This is a great way to utilise your existing apprentices by running Q&A sessions, webinars and you can start a mentoring programme. You can cover areas such as: who to contact if apprentices have concerns, adjusting to learning, learning support, writing reports, and creating and giving presentations for end point assessments.

To support your apprentices and managers, it's recommended you get out into your organisation. Complete overviews with departments and speak to managers to gain an understanding of how apprenticeships can support them. What type of learning do the team already do? Is there a pattern in terms of career paths and the education and training they complete? This can help you highlight where there's a need for apprenticeships; teams may currently pay for training that can be replaced with an apprenticeship standard. You can also use this information to link apprenticeships to career pathways and succession planning.

Take it one step further and each year, spend time with your apprentices, even if it's just for an hour. If you work in a large organisation and are privileged to support hundreds of apprentices, you can still spend some time out and about. You just might not get the time to see every apprentice. You can gather ideas about how to support your apprentices, what's working, what isn't and gather more stories to communicate internally/externally.

Implement apprenticeship events throughout the year. If you're a large organisation and you have the budget, you might arrange a yearly team day e.g. BBQ; you can get everyone together including managers and team mentors. If you're a smaller organisation or you only have a few apprentices, you can facilitate smaller events and they don't need to cost much money. Arrange a breakfast catch-up for an hour, providing juice and pastries. Book a summer and Christmas lunch allowing apprentices to network and give you feedback on the programme. You can even have a "wash up" social at the end of National Apprenticeship Week, thanking apprentices and managers for their input.

Apprenticeship Week

Once you have your trials running smoothly, you can start to plan the future, and one very important event - National Apprenticeship Week . There are various events that you can do during the week (and month) to help you communicate your brand and expand your scheme. Consider:

- Career fairs at local schools and colleges - it's great for brand awareness even if you don't have a vacancy.
- Employability events – working with schools and colleges to run mock interviews and career talks.
- Blogs and videos that you can share internally/externally – have a staggered communication plan for the week/month.
- Using existing apprentices to act as ambassadors, sharing their experiences – potentially launch your apprenticeship champions during National Apprenticeship Week.
- Internal Q&A sessions facilitated by your providers, managers and apprentices.

If you haven't looked at your brand yet, you'll need one for National Apprenticeship Week, and what better way to launch? If you haven't thought about your brand, you might want to implement it at this stage, especially if you attend career fairs. If you're going to attend events, do it properly: brand, promotional material, goodies and in the future...apprentices!

Utilise your apprentices and managers to attend events and fairs with you (you might want to provide some preparation so that they can answer queries about the organisation and reward scheme as well as discuss apprenticeships). Depending on your budget, consider handouts, leaflets, digital resources, banners, videos and branded freebies.

Career fairs are a great opportunity to support the next generation with career and study advice – it can be useful to have colleagues on the stand who have experienced college, university, apprenticeships and workplace study/professional qualifications. You can provide a variety of information to students and parents, helping them make key decisions about their future. University isn't the only option.

Visit GOV.UK to find out about other events and campaigns that are going on throughout the country; there are usually marketing logos that you can use during National Apprenticeship Week and posters/slogans you can share on social media, e.g. the 2019 "Fire It Up" campaign.

Employability Plan

This links to the "Research" chapter where you can start networking with other apprenticeship organisations and experts. This is a great way to find out how you can get more involved with apprenticeships and your local area. Employability is the foundation to your future apprenticeship scheme, focussing on early careers, work experience and promoting your EVP.

Employability comes in many forms, including: career fairs, work experience, manager talks, mock interviews, CV workshops and generally promoting apprenticeships to the wider community. By attending networking events, you'll build contacts from local schools and colleges and you can start to plan your annual events.

Within your area, search for your Local Enterprise Partnership (LEP). The LEP work amongst local authority, education and employers to offer career guidance to students. The LEP can help act as a liaison between your organisation and local education, helping schools achieve the Gatsby Benchmark, ensuring students have regular encounters with employers. The Gatsby Benchmark was created in the 2013 "Good Career Guidance" report, led by Lord Sainsbury and Sir John Holman at the Gatsby Charitable Foundation. The eight benchmarks below, aim to improve the career guidance and support given to students in England:

1. A stable careers programme
2. Learning from career and labour market information
3. Addressing the needs of each pupil
4. Linking curriculum learning to careers
5. Encounters with employers and employees
6. Experiences of workplaces
7. Encounters with further and higher education
8. Personal guidance

You can choose which benchmarks and events you support and link them to your apprenticeship, recruitment and community/charitable giving strategy. Your IT managers could provide talks to IT students. Can students and teachers have a tour of your office and meet apprentices and managers? Can your employees volunteer to help at events, for example, career days? It's recommended you get your trial apprenticeships off the ground before designing your employability plan.

Ambassador Network

Join your area network, which is supported by a variety of areas including employers, LEP and local authority. Their role is to promote and support apprenticeships in the local area. This will help you network with like-minded individuals and you can gain ideas to follow best practice. This could also be a development opportunity for you as well as a chance for your organisation to raise brand awareness. Your involvement in the network will help promote the benefits of apprenticeships to the general public, helping bridge the gap between employers, students, parents, teachers and providers. This links nicely with an employability plan.

Your successful apprentices can also join the YAAN, which is a great way to continue their development. This is aimed at those aged between 16 and 26 and involves attending events and sharing their stories to promote apprenticeships amongst younger age groups. There is also a national and regional network similar to the Apprenticeship Ambassador Network.

Consider this stage once you've given your apprenticeship scheme time to grow so that you can determine where apprenticeships are beneficial in your organisation and how much levy you're likely to spend each year or each cycle. If it's unlikely you'll spend your levy, you can transfer up to 25% of your unused apprenticeship levy to another organisation (you can transfer to more than one employer).

Review the details on the GOV.UK website because this amount may vary depending on the annual budget. You'll also want to familiarise yourself with the funding rules within the employer rules. Key elements are outlined below:

- You can transfer your levy to businesses in your local area, regional partners, employers in completely different industries and ATAs (providing they're registered on the apprenticeship service).
- Funds are deducted monthly; if an apprentice stops, you can simply stop your funds transfer.
- Confirm you can fund the entire apprenticeship duration prior to agreeing a transfer.
- You cannot receive funds if you're providing funds to another employer.
- Funds cannot be transferred to businesses that receive full funding from the government because they have less than 50 employees and are employing an apprentice aged 16 – 18 or 19 – 24 years old.

Speak to your senior leaders to trial a transfer and then you can decide on a plan for the future and build this into your apprenticeship and organisational strategy. It can partner up quite nicely with your charitable and social responsibility strategy. Do you support a charity each year? Do you support local community initiatives? Are there small businesses in your area that are interested in apprenticeships and would benefit from your transfer? Your transfer, for example, could help a small charity recruit a digital apprentice to build their website. Your ambassador network, LEP and local services can help you liaise with organisations who are interested in receiving funds.

Once you've completed your first levy cycle, you'll have the information you need to cement your scheme. Think about the following areas:

- What areas of the organisation were successful with apprenticeships? Consider the interest as well as the impact to the organisation. What impact are you measuring? Is it employee satisfaction and/or performance?
- Have apprenticeships had an impact on attrition and absence rates? This will help you plan your future spending. (If you only trialled a few apprentices, you'll unlikely have the ROI until you've completed several levy cycles).
- If apprenticeships didn't work in certain areas, why not? Do you need to evaluate your communication plan? Is there a culture piece to address?
- How successful were apprenticeship vacancies, both internal and external? Where should levy spending be allocated?

Review every activity from your first levy cycle, right from recruitment and onboarding through to processes and communication. You can see what works and then cement your scheme and build apprenticeships into your everyday culture.

It's important to regularly visit the references within this book to keep abreast of apprenticeship changes and keep updated with the annual apprenticeship employer rules. Changes may also occur to standards and funding based on reactions to the National Audit Office report "The Apprenticeship Programme," (2019).

The cost of apprenticeships were underestimated in the government budget as employers increasingly develop and choose more expensive standards at degree level. There are also concerns whether apprentices meet the 20%

off-the-job training criteria and how the new standards add value to employers. No matter what the government scheme looks like in the future, hopefully this book will enable you to embed apprenticeships into your organisation, building skills, for your organisation, individuals and England.

References

Assets.publishing.service.gov.uk. (2019). *Apprenticeship funding rules and guidance for employers*. [online] Available at: https://assets.publishing.service.gov.uk/government/uploads/system/upload s/attachment_data/file/821577/1920_Employer_Rules_Version_1.0_FINAL.p df [Accessed 01 August. 2019].

GOV.UK. (2019). *Pay Apprenticeship Levy*. [online] Available at: https://www.gov.uk/guidance/pay-apprenticeship-levy [Accessed 2 Jul. 2019].

Great Britain. Apprenticeship Statistics: England (11th February), 2019). *Apprenticeship Statistics: England* Number 06113, 2019 [online]. London: By the authority of the House of Lords. [23rd February 2019]. Available from: file:///C:/Users/natalie.dixey/Downloads/SN06113%20(3).pdf

Oecd.org. (2019). [online] Available at: https://www.oecd.org/education/building-skills-for-all-review-of-england.pdf [Accessed 23 Feb. 2019].

School for startups (2012). *Richard Review of Apprenticeships*. [online] Department for Business, Innovation and Skills. Available at: https://assets.publishing.service.gov.uk/government/uploads/system/upload /attachment_data/file/34708/richard-review-full.pdf [Accessed 28 Feb. 019].

Keen, R. (2019). *A short history of apprenticeships in England: from medieval craft guilds to the twenty-first century.* [online] House of Commons Library. Available at: https://commonslibrary.parliament.uk/economy-business/work-incomes/a-short-history-of-apprenticeships-in-england-from-medieval-craft-guilds-to-the-twenty-first-century/ [Accessed 28 Feb. 2019].

Gov.uk. (2019). *Email alert subscription - GOV.UK.* [online] Available at: https://www.gov.uk/government/email-signup/new?email_signup%5Bfeed%5D=https%3A%2F%2Fwww.gov.uk%2Fgovernment%2Forganisations%2Finstitute-for-apprenticeships.atom [Accessed 29 May. 2019].

GOV.UK. (2019). *How to register and use the apprenticeship service as an employer.* [online] Available at: https://www.gov.uk/guidance/manage-apprenticeship-funds [Accessed 2 Jul. 2019].

Institute for Apprenticeships and Technical Education. (2019). *Home.* [online] Available at: https://www.instituteforapprenticeships.org/ [Accessed 29 May 2019].

Assets.publishing.service.gov.uk. (2019). *The A-Z of apprenticeships.* [online] Available at: https://assets.publishing.service.gov.uk/government/uploads/system/uploac s/attachment_data/file/787716/Apps_Framesworks-150319.pdf [Accessed 29 May 2019].

GOV.UK. (2019). *Apprenticeship agreement: template.* [online] Available at: https://www.gov.uk/government/publications/apprenticeship-agreement-template [Accessed 2 Jul. 2019].

GOV.UK. (2019). *Using the apprenticeship brand.* [online] Available at: https://www.gov.uk/government/publications/using-the-apprenticeship-brand [Accessed 29 May. 2019].

GOV.UK. (2019). *Register of end-point assessment organisations.* [online] Available at: https://www.gov.uk/guidance/register-of-end-point-assessment-organisations [Accessed 29 May. 2019].

Assets.publishing.service.gov.uk. (2019). *Apprenticeship technical funding guide April 2019 – March 2020.* [online] Available at: https://assets.publishing.service.gov.uk/government/uploads/system/upload s/attachment_data/file/795249/Apprenticeships_technical_funding_guide_2 019_to_2020_V1_April2019.pdf [Accessed 2 Jul. 2019].

GOV.UK. (2019). *Complaints procedure.* [online] Available at: https://www.gov.uk/government/organisations/institute-for-apprenticeships/about/complaints-procedure [Accessed 29 May 2019].

Adzuna. (2019). *28,604 Apprenticeships Jobs in the UK | Adzuna.* [online] Available at: https://www.adzuna.co.uk/jobs/apprenticeships [Accessed 1 Jul. 2019].

GOV.UK. (2019). *Become an apprentice*. [online] Available at:
https://www.gov.uk/apprenticeships-guide/pay-and-conditions [Accessed 12
Jun. 2019].

GOV.UK. (2019). *Employer National Insurance contributions for apprentices
under 25*. [online] Available at:
https://www.gov.uk/government/publications/national-insurance-
contributions-for-under-25s-employer-guide [Accessed 29 May 2019].

YAAN. (2019). *The Young Apprentice Ambassador Network | YAAN |
Homepage*. [online] Available at: https://amazingapprenticeships.com/yaan/
[Accessed 5 May 2019].

GOV.UK. (2019). *Transferring unused apprenticeship funds to other
employers*. [online] Available at: https://www.gov.uk/guidance/transferring-
apprenticeship-service-funds [Accessed 5 May 2019].

Lepnetwork.net. (2019). *The LEP Network | Supporting all 38 LEPs across
England*. [online] Available at: https://www.lepnetwork.net/ [Accessed 19
June. 2019].

The Gatsby Charitable Foundation (2019). *Good Career Guidance*. [online]
The Gatsby Charitable Foundation. Available at:
https://www.gatsby.org.uk/uploads/education/reports/pdf/gatsby-sir-john-
holman-good-career-guidance-2014.pdf [Accessed 19 Jun. 2019].

Assets.publishing.service.gov.uk. (2019). *Employer Rules*. [online] Available at:
https://assets.publishing.service.gov.uk/government/uploads/system/upload s/attachment_data/file/814514/1920_Employer_Rules_v1.0_FINAL__clarific ation_version_.pdf [Accessed 6 Jul. 2019].

Department for Education (2019). *The Apprenticeship Programme*. [online] National Audit Office. Available at: https://www.nao.org.uk/wp-content/uploads/2019/03/The-apprenticeships-programme.pdf [Accessed 7 Jul. 2019].

Printed in Great Britain
by Amazon

44748543R00052